KT-375-036

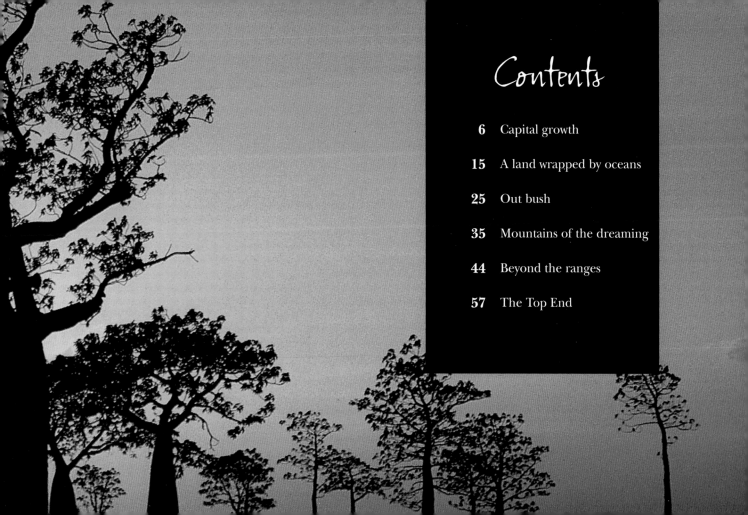

Contents

At the age of sixteen, I began to photograph my Australian discoveries, in those days primarily under water. At the age of thirty, I emerged from the sea to record the land and its flora and fauna. During my travels, I met such interesting people leading such interesting lives that I began to photograph them, too.

Australia is amazingly unusual in many ways. There is a multitude of habitats from tropical rainforests to alpine peaks, the wildlife is unique and abundant, and the people are colourful and friendly. So, having experienced the joy of photographing Australia for forty years now, I do hope this book and its associated CD-ROM give you a sense of the magic that is, to me, Australia.

Steve Parish

CAPITAL GROWTH

Each of Australia's cities has its own, very distinct identity. Apart from the glass towers that seem an inescapable part of every CBD, architecture has developed differently in each capital. Local people have their own ways of speaking and of welcoming strangers, and the pace of life differs in each city.

As a photographer, I have spent long days "street-walking" in every one of them in search of images.

On every visit to any particular city I notice change – not just the obvious changes in the skyline and on building sites, but more subtle changes in the public attitudes, acceptances and enterprises of the city's residents.

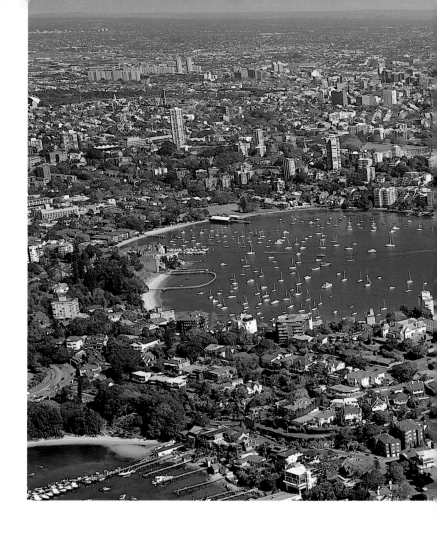

Looking across Sydney Harbour from Point Piper to the city.

The lights of Adelaide's CBD reflect in Torrens Lake.

The Story Bridge etched against the CBD, Brisbane, Queensland.

Looking across Perth Water on the Swan River to Perth city, WA.

Anzac Avenue, Canberra, leading to Australia's Parliament House.

Wrest Point Casino on Sandy Bay, Hobart, Tasmania.

An aerial shot of Darwin, Northern Territory, and its harbour.

Looking from The Spit over the Broadwater and south to Main Beach and Surfers Paradise, Gold Coast, Queensland.

TO SURRENDER *totally to a seascape, I need to be enveloped in the glow of dawn or dusk, at one with nature and with myself. Without any distractions, I can forget self and enjoy the peace that the ocean brings me. Few things can match the beauty of a sea, normally wild and clamorous, when it is gentle and at peace, burnished ripplets merging with the silvered gold light of the sinking sun. This shot of the Twelve Apostles is one of my favourites, and I feel again the calm of that golden afternoon whenever I look at it.*

Looking from The Spit over the Broadwater and south to Main Beach and Surfers Paradise, Gold Coast, Queensland.

Sunset over Cable Beach, Broome, Western Australia, and a string of camels quietly paces the shore.

There are countless spots along Australia's lengthy coastline where a watcher can meditate on the sea's ever-changing moods. I can find fulfilment on sweeping sandy beaches, rocky headlands where waves crash on the cliffs below, coral atolls or mudflats that glisten as the tide retreats. I have even felt my heart lighten in a tropical mangrove forest, where the silence was broken only by mysterious snappings and bubblings.

The closer I am to the ocean, the more powerfully I am affected. This transformation of the soul has been recorded by others in poetry and prose, pictured in oils, watercolour, charcoal and ink, even captured in music. In Australia, the sea coast is free to all, and we can all be moved by the ancient magic of the ocean.

TO SURRENDER *totally to*

a seascape, I need to be enveloped in the

glow of dawn or dusk, at one with

nature and with myself. Without any

distractions, I can forget self and enjoy

the peace that the ocean brings me. Few

things can match the beauty of a sea,

normally wild and clamorous, when it is

gentle and at peace, burnished ripplets

merging with the silvered gold light of

the sinking sun. This shot of the Twelve

Apostles is one of my favourites, and I

feel again the calm of that golden

afternoon whenever I look at it.

The Twelve Apostles bathed in gold, Port Campbell National Park, Victoria.

A glowing coral garden with its myriad attendant fishes in the World Heritage listed Great Barrier Reef Marine Park, Queensland.

An Orange-fin Anemonefish shelters among the tentacles of its anemone.

The view of a seashore at sunrise or sunset does wonderful things for the human spirit.

Relieving the tension of the workaday world.

THOUSANDS *of city-stressed people use the magic of the sea to shift their tensions.*

Even in the crowds at a popular beach, I can create my own space and wander, enclosed in my own meditative capsule, along the edge of the water.

Minutes have a habit of turning to hours, and days to weeks, in these places. There are footprints to make, mysteries to unravel, feathers, shells and strange plants to discover, and barely visible tracks to follow.

The bathing-boxes at Brighton, Victoria, crowd together, as bright and fresh as Toytown.

Sydney's beaches (above right) always seem to have room for one more.

OUT OF NINETEEN MILLION *Australians, more than 90 per cent live within a hundred kilometres of Australia's seven-thousand kilometre coastline. Small wonder, then, that as Australia swelters in the summer, the sea is the nation's number one playground. On hot and sultry days, hundreds of thousands visit any of a thousand beaches for a cooling dip.*

Mountain Ash and tree ferns, Dandenong Ranges National Park, Victoria.

OUT BUSH

What is "the bush"? For me it is everywhere, be it coastal heath, mallee, tall eucalypt forest or its scraggly cousin of the tropical north. The bush has trees and shrubs, and it is home to wild creatures whose survival depends on evading the fangs and claws of their fellows, and on coping with periods of feast and famine as dictated by uncertain rainfall.

When I go bush, I try to pack plenty of patience, persistence and adaptability. I take on the ways of the bush, the most important of which is: do not hurry – stop, look at and listen to every thing around.

The bush is still an important part of Australia's folklore – the continuing popularity of "Waltzing Matilda" bears testimony to that.

The Koala, at home in the eucalypt forests.

A young Emu, not far from maturity.

A Red-necked Wallaby, alert in tall grass.

The Laughing Kookaburra, inhabitant of the bush.

Leading out the mob: drovers work cattle along a stock route in Queensland's Gulf Country.

Shearing the wethers, the board satiny with lanolin from the wool.

Wattle grows in all bush habitats from desert to coast.

Towering gums characterise the Australian bush.

Delicate flowering eucalypts ornament the bush.

Late afternoon sun slants through River Red Gums on the banks of the Darling, New South Wales.

Finches, robins and wrens all shelter in long grass, shrubs and reeds – finding them is hard!

Near Katoomba, the Three Sisters jut out from the sandstone cliffs above the Jamison Valley in the Blue Mountains, New South Wales.

As a child, I loved mountains. I would wander for hours in the Mount Lofty Ranges behind Adelaide after I had escaped with my dog from "all those awful adults". Having reached a suitable spur of rock, I would sit for hours, staring out across the city to the sea, my dog sleeping at my side. The fascination is with me still, and it is shared by many other Australians.

Australia's Great Dividing Range, with its many offshoots, runs continuously from the tip of Cape York for over 2400 kilometres to the Grampians in Central Victoria. The peaks and valleys vary enormously from the north's tropical rainforest to the alpine peaks of the south. Toowoomba, in Southern Queensland, is the only city on the Great Divide.

Bone-snappingly cold water tumbles between snow-covered rocks.

Clouds drift across a snow-clad peak in Mt Kosciuszko National Park, Australian Alps, New South Wales.

Stirling Range, south-west Western Australia, etched against a dawn sky.

A horseman from Tom Groggin Station crosses the upper Murray River.

A female Eclectus Parrot from northern rainforests.

Chalahn Falls, Lamington National Park, southern Queensland.

The Red-eyed Tree-frog lives high in the forest canopy.

MOUNTAINS *clad in rainforest are home to some of Australia's most unique and endangered birds, animals and plants. But rainforest does not share its secrets readily – it is one of the hardest locations for photography.*

Mountains are also the birthplace of many rivers; some, like the mighty Murray, have been heavily exploited since first settled by Europeans.

Tchupala Falls, Wooroonooran National Park, north Queensland.

Russell Falls, Mount Field National Park, Tasmania.

A rainforest creek, Daintree National Park, north Queensland.

*There is something very special about the
arid lands of central Australia. I am
lured back time and time again. I love
the red dunes draped in rare wildflowers,
the rocky escarpments dotted with spiky
spinifex, the swaying, golden grasses of
the plains, the waterholes and dry creeks
lined with drooping River Red Gums,
the sun reflecting from the gibber plains.
This is an ancient world, a land of red
dirt and blue sky, at its most spectacular
when storm clouds from the west move
east to overpower the blue with towering
castles of grey-black that will flush
vermilion as the sun sets.*

Uluru, the great red rock at a nation's heart, framed by Desert Oaks.

Cattlemen move a mob through the dust and haze of the plains.

Amateur jockeys take time to play, urging the runners home at a country race meeting.

The sandhills of the Centre bloom after rain.

Flower of a *Parakeelya* species, or "bush portulaca" (above right).

WHENEVER *rain falls and water flows across the dunes and plains Outback, a carpet of living colour will soon follow... The flowering scrub trees, shrubs and ground plants burst forth with a riotous array of yellows, reds, mauves, lilacs, oranges and vivid pinks, offset by delicate white and cream.*

Paper daisies and other wildflowers surround a claypan in the Rainbow Valley Conservation Area of the Northern Territory.

AUSTRALIANS *are proud of their bush heritage and, in many towns, small and large, hard work is going into restoring and retaining remnants of the past. Outback pubs are perhaps the most popular, but there are also churches, cottages and homesteads, and, along the Murray, old paddle-steamers have been lovingly restored.*

The *Emmylou* paddles by on the River Murray (above left).

The Silverton Hotel in New South Wales flies the Australian flag, remote from the bustle of the modern mining industry at its near neighbour, Broken Hill.

The Pinnacles, Nambung National Park, Western Australia – pillars of limestone dredged from the sand by ceaseless wind.

Chambers Pillar, a weathered remnant south of Alice Springs, Northern Territory.

Florence Falls in beautiful Litchfield National Park in the Northern Territory's north west.

THE TOP END

The landscapes, fauna and flora of the tropical Top End of the Northern Territory are among the most breathtaking in Australia. The tropical monsoons, which announce themselves each year in black clouds crackling with lightning, create wetland environments that support a profusion of living things, and bring much-needed water to the stone country of the escarpment. The annual cyclonic rains support multitudes of mammals, birds, reptiles, frogs and invertebrates, while the seas teem with marine life.

This abundance of natural food supported indigenous people across the continent's north for tens of thousands of years; in some areas it supports them still.

I can think of no better place to be a photographer.

One of the galleries around Nourlangie Rock, Kakadu National Park.

Twin Falls in flood, Kakadu National Park.

An Azure Kingfisher perched above a waterhole, eyes alert.

The exquisite Lotus, one of the most beautiful food sources in the world.

A flock of Australian Pelicans soar over the floodplains of Kakadu.

A Jabiru (Black-necked Stork) preening its wing feathers.

THE STEVE PARISH · AUSTRALIA FROM THE HEART COLLECTION

ALSO IN THE SAME SERIES:

Wild Places • Wildlife • Brisbane • Melbourne • Sydney

WHY NOT VISIT OUR WEBSITE FOR FURTHER DETAILS?

www.steveparish.com.au

Australia from the Heart

INTERACTIVE CD-ROM

If you have enjoyed Steve's magnificent book about Australia, and would like more, we suggest that you look at the exciting Australia CD-ROM packed with his brilliant images.

Over 150 stunning pictures are featured in:

• an interactive STORYBOOK that will take you further into this wonderful country

• a breathtaking SLIDE SHOW set to music

• PHOTOGRAPHIC TIPS to help you make glorious landscape and natural history pictures of your own

• CLIP ART to decorate your e-mails and stationery, create your own greeting cards, or illustrate school projects

• DESKTOP PICTURES that will transform your computer screen

• a SCREEN SAVER picture show

• ELECTRONIC GREETING CARDS

• Steve's own story in MEET STEVE PARISH.

The CD-ROM is both Mac and IBM compatible, and comes with a free download of Quicktime Player 5.

From an early age, Steve Parish has been driven by his undying passion for Australia to photograph every aspect of it, from its wild animals and plants to its many wild places. Then he began to turn his camera on Australians and their ways of life. This body of work forms one of Australia's most diverse photographic libraries. Over the years, these images of Australia have been used in thousands of publications, from cards, calendars and stationery to books – pictorial, reference, guide and children's. Steve has combined his considerable talents as a photographer, writer, poet and public speaker with his acute sense of needs in the marketplace to create a publishing company that today is recognised world wide.

Steve's primary goal is to turn the world on to nature, and, in pursuit of this lifelong objective, he has published a world-class range of children's books and learning aids. He sees our children as the decision makers of tomorrow and the guardians of our heritage.

Steve Parish
PUBLISHING

Published by Steve Parish Publishing Pty Ltd

PO Box 1058, Archerfield, Queensland 4108 Australia

www.steveparish.com.au

© copyright Steve Parish Publishing Pty Ltd

ISBN 1 74021 081 6

All rights reserved. No part of this publication may be reproduced, stored in a retrieval system, or transmitted in any form or by any means, electronic, mechanical, photocopying, recording or otherwise, without the prior permission in writing of the Publisher.

Photography & text: Steve Parish

Photos: p. 1, Koala; p. 2, Boabs on the Kimberley plains; pp. 4–5, Magpie Geese on a Top End wetland

Cover design: Audra Colless

Printed in Hong Kong by South China Printing Co. Ltd

Film by Vakta, Pty Ltd, Australia

Designed and produced in Australia at the Steve Parish Publishing Studios